POEMS

POEMS

Writings from My Youth
Written by Tom Fahey
Inspired by Kathy Fahey

"POEMS" copyright 2022 by Thomas Fahey
Published by Thomas Fahey

FIRST EDITION

For my wife Kathy,

My love, my inspiration, pushing me to write, and buoying my spirit through the years.

Thank you.

Poems
Rough Draft
Finished Copy

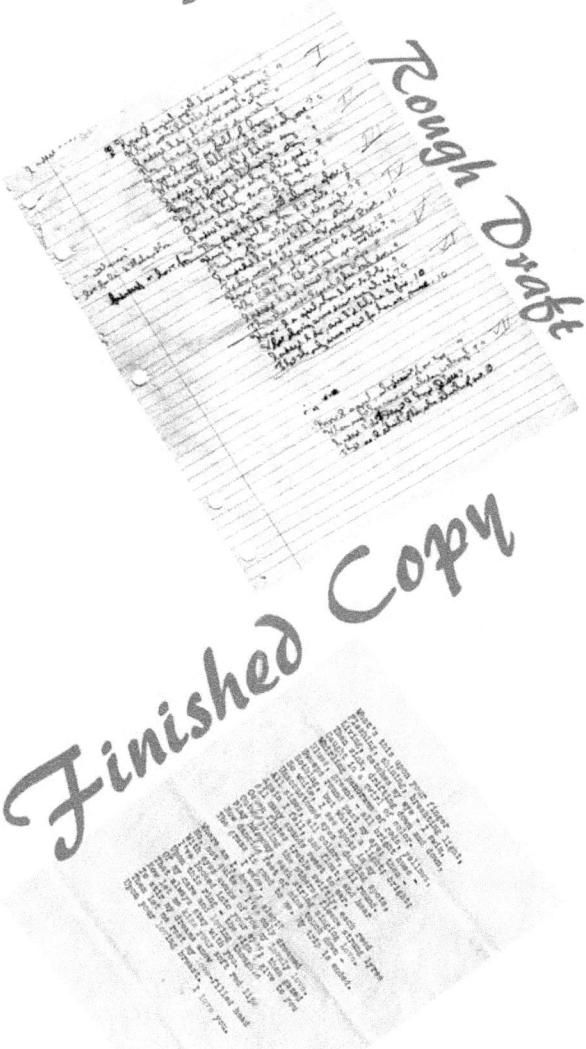

WHY I WRITE

In the fourth grade I wore my best white sailboat-print shirt. My bright blue eyes, highlighted by white hair flopping down on my brown freckle-speckled face, stare straight ahead into the photographer's square, black camera. My large gap-toothed grin fills this year's school picture, belying my true reticent nature.

I wasn't always shy. Until sometime in fourth grade, my school progress reports were peppered with checkmarks—"Exercises self-control." I loved to talk; talking to anyone who'd listen until one fateful afternoon. Seated back row of room five, I chinwag cute little Loretta Kelly.

The hair on the back of my neck bristles as someone grabs my shirt collar, twists it, and screams, "Thomas, shut up!" I squirm, but she pulls me up from my seat and yells again. "I don't want to hear another sound out of you." Still holding onto a piece of my collar, Miss Pancera leads me from my desk to the coat room cohabitated by galoshes, umbrellas and rain coats—no fourth graders except for me. She tells me to stay right there. My eyes open wide but my body stiffens. She returns dragging my desk behind her. She urges me to sit in that desk and orders, "Don't talk. Don't move from this desk until I tell you to do so."

Well, I was known to be chatty, never stupid. She did not have to tell me twice. I understood that sitting in the coat room by myself stood at the bottom of the fourth-grade totem of esteem. In response my hackles hardened and my ears seared red with mule-like determination. "I'll show her. I'll show everyone. I won't ever talk again." And I didn't.

Teachers now thought me to be a cute, shy young man. I played this charade as I slunk back into my quiet shell. I could wait until recess or even after school to do a little yelling, screaming, or just chit-chatting. I adapted.

As I quietly began eighth grade something changed. An enthusiastic young teacher fresh from college stirred my inner muse. She introduced the class to the excitement of literature. She began class each day enjoining us to read aloud Henry Wadsworth Longfellow's 'Evangeline: A Tale of Acadie.'

> This is the forest primeval. Murmuring pines and hemlocks,
> Bearded with moss, in garments green, indistinct in the twiligt
> Stand like Druids of eld, with voices sad and prophetic,
> Stand like harpers hoar, with beards that rest on their bosoms.
> Loud from its rocky caverns, the deep-voiced neighboring ocean
> Speaks, in accents disconsolate answers the wail of the forest...

*Ye who believe affection that hopes, and endures, and is patient
Ye who believe in the beauty and strength of woman's devotion,
List to the mournful tradition, sung by the pines of the forest;
List to a Tale of Love in Acadie, home of the happy.'*

Each day a new chapter to Evangeline's 'tale of love' decanted a new draught of word portraits overflowing my stein of senses. Hooked, I dropped Penrod, Homer Price, The Hardy Boys off my library list. I yearned for real literature. A whole new world of sights, sounds, feelings opened to me. I wanted to read. I soon devoured everything my eyes attacked.

I no longer needed to talk; I needed to read, to listen and then to write. This young eighth-grade teacher Miss Schmidt encouraged me to write. She thought I had a talent for writing. My voice, once manacled in the fourth grade coat room, unleashed itself with number-two pencil married to college-ruled paper. With things to say, I no longer feared the tug on my shirt collar. I could write to be heard.

Calendar pages flipped over and over like leaves of Fall. I continued to write. In between bouts of kneeling on my hands for talking and goofing off, I asked high school English teacher Father Elliot how I could improve my literary style. He told me to be quiet, to keep from trouble, and to stay after school to write for the Roger Bacon Yearbook. I mostly heeded that advice, taking to heart his pejorative urging, "Write what you know."

Junior year a youthful infatuation died and Phoenix-like I climbed from the ashes to a full-time, long-term relationship promising roses and romance. Puppy-loved Ann Honnert tipped me over but kindly poured me out and back into the dating teapot with Kathy Eder. I went from desolate and dateless to arm around this brunette in the backseat of a '56 Chevy en route to McAuley's Junior Prom.

A bumpy, pot-holed start eventually smoothed to a lengthy relationship spawning an abundance of inspiration for my creative soul. Thus, the big reveal of the following pages unfold—a rescued raft of poems written from what I felt and what I knew about myself and the lovely young girl who became the love of my life, Kay Fahey. A metered, rhyming name like that had to be glorified in iambic pentameter.

Poems followed Tom and Kay from high school, through college, into marriage and our early life together. They bear no resemblance to literary excellence, but they are truly a reflection of heart-felt emotions. Father Elliot said to write what I know. Love for Kay is what I felt, what I knew. Blame it on him, but enjoy anyway.

Poet

August 14, 1964

I'm no poet
Don't you know it,
But even so
I'll go real slow
And try to write
To you tonight.
These wishes of mine
That you're just fine,
And whatever you do
Remember I miss you

                 Your little pet dinosaur.

One Year Ago

March 1965

One year ago I first met you.
Now all my plans are made for two.
Never did I know I'd find
You'd be the girl I'd want as mine.
First you duped me with your charms,
Then I fell into your arms.
Now I guess you think you're smart,
For you have also caught my heart.

The lovely pink dress that you first wore,
Your funny ways that I adore,
Those wondrous nights upon the phone,
The words you spoke for me alone.
Coney Island and all its fun,
That lucky star you wished upon,
The times we got quite serious,
A tree and dreams of happiness,
Your warm hand for me to hold,
Those tender kisses that we stole,
All helped to make one happy year
That in my heart I held so dear.

Words from the Golf Course

Here I sit pen in hand

Hoping you will understand

Just how hard it is to write

Sitting in the hot sunlight.

I'm just fine, hope you're the same.

Sure do miss you, 'What's your name?'

Whatcha' doing? Having fun?

I'm still sweating in the searing sun.

This poem may be a little sloppy,

But at least it a'int a carbon-copy.

Cause even with all the things I do,

I can't help but kinda' think of you.

Tell Me

Kan you tell me why it are
All I do is gawk afar?
Yet my dreams don't take me thar.
I never asked much of stars.

Love is what I want and need.
Only no one seems to hear me plead
Very sad on bended knee
Each night that you are not with me.

Yes, I beg that you'll be mine
Over and over do I pine
U I want all the time.

Lovely Pink Dress

June, 1965

The lovely pink dress that you first wore,

Your funny ways that I adore,

Those wonderful nights upon the phone,

The words you spoke to me alone,

Coney Island and all its fun,

The lucky star we wished upon,

Your soft, sweet hand for me to hold,

Those tender kisses that we stole,

The times we got quite serious,

A tree and dreams of happiness,

All helped to make one happy year

That in my heart I'll hold so dear.

Lonely Room

December 17, 1965

Lonely room where I stay
    Tell her of my tortured thought.
Tear-stained bed where I lay
    Whisper those words I dare not.
Consoling pillow where I dream
    Tell her of my restless night.
Sleepy sheets where tears stream
    Reveal to her my soul's dear flight.

Listless lips that ever mourn
    Tell her of my passion's strength.
Empty heart that seeks a home
    Cry to her my longing's length.
Whisper do these mournful lines
    For I won't rest till she is mine.

Albers Supermarket

September 11, 1968
The Burma-Shave-like signs atop the dairy case read, " Barney Kroger has biscuits too, but only Albers has a poem for you."

TomFahey

How do I love thee?

Let me count the ways.

I love thee to the depth and

The breadth of thy gleaming stockrooms.

To the one-stroked floors

Of thy spacious meat rooms—

To the fragrant walls

Of they glowing restrooms.

I love thee so, my heart ov'r flowing

With grandiose yearning

For more of thy cheering warmth.

I love thee, I hate to part

Your singing resisters.

I hate to say good-bye

To the music of your happy people.

I hate to tear away

From all your beauteous parts.

But woe is me!
Alas! Alack!
A pox on the cold wind
That smacks my face when'ere
I leave thy towering portals.

It is only a deep, burning,
Never ending, always yearning,
Longing for your blessed
Coins dropped from skies on Fridays
That keeps me; but what a
Strong tie that is.

Yes, Albers, I do love thee
To the depth and the breadth
Of thy gleaming stockrooms—
But never ask me why.

Only time and God
Will know or tell why
My heart to thee is tied.

Words

The only words you need to say
Are 'Please do show to me the way.'
I'll take your tender hand in mine
And fly you softly to could nine.
Then I'll begin my pleasant task
Doing whatever you might ask.
From villain's dungeon I would wrest
You, fair damsel, in distress.
I'll waken my brown-tressed beauteous miss
From an evil spell with one sweet kiss.
Each night I'll steal my brown-eyed maid
With my soft-sung serenade.
I'll write an epic of her charms
And love that waits within her arms.
With one fell swoop I'll down the foe
Who dares to speak of my love so.
For my sweet Queen I'll off to fight
Not coming home till wrong is right.
But soon I'm sure I will return
To this one girl for whom I yearn.
Then learning that she too loves me
I'll ask she, 'Will you marry me?'

Gone

Dearest love you've gone from here,
My arms hold only lifeless air.
My lips taste only bitter smoke.
My eyes see only words I wrote.

Sweet girl your face bursts ope' my soul
With fire and fury uncontrolled,
With searing flames tears cannot drench.
With withering thirst words cannot quench.

Soft words you say soothe my soul's heat,
Yet on my face blows no breath sweet,
Yet over the crowds are your words tossed,
Yet in the crowds are your words lost.

Lost love return to within my reach
That tween our hearts no thing may breach.

Love
January 1969

Love is a people-thing/ I know.
I have experienced it, but
Only part and incomplete.
Yet even so I feel its power
Swell and grow within me.
Indeed, it grows but once twas not.
It did not grow in me.
Hate, time, then understanding brought love
To my heart and peace to my soul.

Now with time I pray your hate has
Ceased and understanding comes to you,
So that you may enjoy the peace
That love brings to all.
Love your fellow man and learn
Love does not come easy to all.
You must show your love first
That all may reap its fruits
And live forever with knowledge that,
Love is a people thing.

Monday Morning

Monday morning at six a.m.
Kiss wife and baby good-bye.
Up the stairs, out the door
Into the blue two-door sedan,
Close the door, roll the window tight,
Step on the gas, smell the fumes.

You're dead.
Rise up, climb out of the coffin,
You're renewed, you're revived,
You live again, you are called
To a life, a trip.
Only you hold the key.

 Turn it, open the door, dive in.
The bright shining, clear shimmering pool
Carries you on currents through wonderful,
Psychedelic, broken, bending, exciting.
What a high spirit this pool emotes,
That between tall canyoned walls of glass.

Cut and glittering green, red, yellow, paisley
Rising, climbing high above the eye's reach,
Dropping straight and forever into the pool.
Change course, steer from the canyon
Onto earth's dense, flowered, fruited garden.
Pluck a plum, a pear, a peach, delicious.

Rise up, climb out of the coffin.
You are renewed. You are revived.
You live again.
To a life, a trip.

Thoughts

Silent paper, my only friend
You alone have known my heart
With you my sweet secrets end
And no one else will read my thoughts.

But wait! There's one with whom I wish
To share my self completely;
Yet not with words, only a kiss
Can I give to her my thoughts.

Please pure friend, tell her please,
How she so obssesses me.
On your blue lines carry my pleas
And give to her my thoughts.

If only you would speak for me
Those words my mouth imprisons,
Her heart could not but help to see
My heart, my soul, my thoughts.

But you like me are silent;
My thoughts you can't reveal.
So now I live in torment
Til my dear knows my thoughts.

My thoughts are of her only,
These dreams that sleep within.
It's Kay I long to marry.
It's she concerns my thoughts.

Let Me Not

Let me not love you my dear
Less I be led away,
From world by words you say
In sweet convincing ways.

Let me not love you my dear
Should you my heart dismiss
With one unfaithful kiss
That seeks for soul not lips.

Let me not love you my dear
Lest I should chance to see
This beauty that is thee,
Which has thus tempted me.

Let me not love you my dear
If you should fill my ear
With words I dare not hear
Whenever you are near.

Let me not love you at all,
Yet may I love you still.
For I know not my will
You have my mind so thrilled
That I must love you still.

Glimmering Star

Like the glimmering star you wish upon
You're far so far from me.
I've need of words for you alone;
But I just can't make you see.

How very much I think of you
Not now, but every day.
There's time I feel so very blue;
You just don't know my way.

I try, no one knows how I try
To tell you about your kiss;
I start, you don't hear, I cry,
Things always go amiss.

Once I hurt you—never again;
Can't you see I like you so.
But you never understand.
You know I'll never go.

A day ago I longed to kiss you,
But I hold that old memory.
So I want to do what you'd like me to;
How I'd hoped you'd only see.

Remember, this was written after I returned home
after Bacon's play a couple weeks ago.

Song of Love

Sing a song of love to her,
Sweet melody to charm her heart
With soft refrains weave magic sounds
To tenderly stir her heart.

Breathe nectar's notes, tunes of joy
That lure her to my lips;
Then go but more an octave higher
And sing to her my kiss.

Beg her to come near to me.
'Pray listen closely dear,
It's not my heart's slow beat,
But it's my love you hear.'

Yes, listen to my love,
To its song pay heed,
'Your heart alone is what I want,
Your love is what I need.'

Listen not to my heart's tune
For songs are writ by fools;
Listen only to the boy—
'I love you.'

At Your Door

Here I am at your door
Telling you just once more,
How I'd very like to be
With you eternally.

Now to you these words I've told,
Then the car door I will hold,
Hoping you will step inside
And scoot closer to my side.

Aha! I.ve got you by my side,
Now from my arms just try to hide.
I've caught you for all time I pray;
If not, then only the rest of today.

Everything

Everything I have to give
Is yours as long as I shall live;
My arms to tenderly enfold,
And keep my dear within their hold.

My lips to warm you with a kiss,
And fill your heart with happiness.
My hand to brush away your tears,
And hold you near over the years.

My dreams to share with only you,
And plan a life for just we two.
My heart and all its precious love
With heavenly blessings from above.

With You

With you I live.
With you I die.
For you I smile.
For you I cry.

The shadows of night crowd across my room,
Yet I sit alone and pray.
No other words dare cross my lips,
Yet I sit alone and say.

With you I live.
With you I die.
For you I laugh.
For you I sigh.

Now I give you my self
For you to use as you wish.
Yet, treat me gentle as a babe,
For whom you save your tender kiss.

To you my heart.
To you my years.
For you my dreams.
For you my tears.

No Reason

You've no reason to stay with me.
I'm young, green , a lot to see.
No success have I gained.
Life's plan before me get to be laid.

One little thing begs you to stay-
Love growing stronger each passing day.
But, love unreturned makes life incomplete-
I beg for your heart both tender and sweet.

If we share a love so holy and good,
I'm sure our lives will be all they should.
My dreams are all built on castles of sand,
But with you they'll be all that they should.

If you'll stay with me the rest of my hours,
Every dream I have will soon become ours.

How?

How can a boy live in two different worlds—
A time of hate and of love,
His only hope from up above
That he shall have a love?

How can a boy live in two different worlds—
Seeing but not knowing why,
His is to do and to die
For freedom he cannot deny?

How can a boy live in two different worlds—
Loving but not being free,
His only wish being to see
This girl will his alone be?

How can a boy live in two different worlds—
Living but not being alive,
His only goal being to strive
To have this girl be his bride?

How can a boy live in two different worlds—
Dreaming yet being afraid,
That some how plans so well laid
Will fail and I'll lose my dear Kay?

Land of Dreams

Somewhere a land of dreams come true
Is waiting just for you.
Only words you need to say
'Show me where Tom Fahey.'

I'd take your tender hand in mine
And fly you to cloud number nine.
Then I'd begin my pleasant task
Doing anything that you should ask.

From the dreaded dragon I would wrest
My fair damsel from distress.
I'd waken my brown-tressed lovely miss
From evil spell with just one kiss.

Each night I'd steal my brown-eyed maid
With my softly sung serenade.
I'd pen an epic bout her charms
And the love she holds within her arms.

With one fell swoop I'd down the foe
Who dared speak of my loved one so.
For my sweet queen I'd off to fight
Not coming home till wrong was right.

But soon I'm sure I would return
To earth and the girl for whom I yearn.
Then learning that she too loved me
I'd ask if she would marry me.

Time

April 6, 1967
(An irregular little piece of trivia composed while hovering on the sheets a foot above my floor while travelling from here to nowhere on my Springtime thoughts of love and Kay.)

Time is such a fine thing to use,
Yet it's quite a finer thing to waste-
Fiddling and doodling and thinking of you.
(But it's terrible my brain turns to paste.)

Spring's at my window tapping the pane,
Even though it's dark, cold, and it's wet.
Such a pity I should stuff my brain
With trivia I will soon forget.

I hear birds in my brain, at the sun I look,
And I do think I must be bezerk.
My hands are too weak to open a book,
And I can't seem to make myself work.

Don't think I'm crying ove' work not worked,
I need not be pitied for this.
It's just that I've such an odd quirk
Brought on by the thought of your kiss.

Really I don't mind being lazy at all;
How else could I be able to find
All the time for the big thoughts so small
That run round my head tickling my mind.

It's too late for Spring to go run and hide;
I've seen her, I'm set to attack.
First I'll bring her to be by my side
Then beg her go into her act.

Put it on! Put it on! All yer bright green.
Dance yer flowers round and round my head.
Sneak into my head where we'll not be seen,
And kiss me, I will not bloom red.

Better still sweet Spring act no go-between.
Dance my love in front of my head.
She'll sneak where we'll not be seen
And kiss me, I will not bloom red.

Know I a Girl

Know I a girl with hair so brown,
Whose voice that like an angel sounds?
Indeed I do, I've no need to shout,
Nay, her tune I can't do without.

Know I a girl so full of fun,
Whose smile says 'she's the only one?'
Indeed I do, and I'd like to say
Near her always I hope to stay.

Know I a girl who when she's sad,
Asks me tearfully 'make me glad?'
Indeed I do, doesn't she know
My eyes for her will always glow.

Know I a girl for whom I'd write,
Thinking of her all thru the night?
Indeed I do, and I'll ever strive
Find words for that gem on Woodview Drive.

Know I a girl who alone I'd kiss,
Who fills my life with joy and bliss?
Indeed I do, need I say more
Then the words I speak at her back door.

Know I a girl whom I love to hold,
Whose loving arms drive way the cold?
Indeed I do, and I'd like her to find
That the only arms for her should be mine.

Know I a girl, who dreams of me too
When night has come and day is through?
Indeed I do, and I hope she'll see
As I think of her, so she thinks of me.

A Tree

For you I'd climb the mountains high,

I'd gather stars up in the sky;

But I'd rather stay put on the ground

Build a tree house for the girl I've found.

I'd work so hard throughout the day

Make it perfect for my dear Kay.

Then one day that tree I'd climb

Only to spend the rest of time

With lovely you sitting at my feet

And me to stroke your head so sweet.

You're the only girl you see

  With whom I'd love to share a tree.

Could This Be?

Could this be my heart you've got
Swinging from a tree,
Dreaming all the while of you
And just how things may be?
Certainly no one else does this
That to me you do;
Then I've never met a girl
Who's quite the same as you.
Nothing makes me happier
Then your pleasing smile;
It's only you makes me good,
Who makes things so worthwhile.
It's only you makes me do
The very best I can;
Someday it will be my pleasure
To ask you for your hand.

I've Thought

I've thought a lot the whole week through,

And I believe I'm fonder of you.

I imagine you find me hard to see,

My feelings turn so easily.

I think I know what I need,

Now please my words take heed.

Maybe I would try a little more,

If I need beat someone else to your door.

Can't Help Thinking

Can't help thinking the world of you;
I'm sure my feelings must show through.
But if they don't, I'm here to say
'I hope to make you mine some day.'
The loveliest girl so I've been told,
Has not only beauty to behold;
But like you, I seem to find,
Is pure and good and sweet and kind.
For this I like you more and more
Each time we kiss at your front door.
I'd like to see the world's great plan
Just to see where we will stand;
Together, I hope, but who can see
Till then I'll pray you'll be with me.
For now I know what I'd like to do;
Spend my whole life pleasing you.

May this be your best birthday ever
With much, much happiness for you.
May you see a tear shed never,
Over dreams that didn't come true.

Love II

April 16, 1978

Love is ours, we've shared it
Through good and bad and all
That could have bid us quit.
But here we are as one,
Forever, I've no doubt.
We've begun again new
Each time and without
The urge and push of any,
Except our own strong will.
We need nothing but each
Other to choose yet still,
To be in perfect union.

You are mine, I've loved it
In winter and in spring.
My hands in yours do fit.
I will not break this hold,
But grasp more tightly to
The one who gives me strength,

Also peace, love, hope—you.
Your virtue surges through me
Whenever we should touch.
So is your loving way
Tjat I feel in you so much—
The closeness that I need.

So ours is love we've shared,
We've given much to each;
And found a gift so rare
As only we could know.
What more can we do now
Than continue to share
And our most vital gift sow
Onto our furrowed fields
Then in our loving give
The gift we've offered each
To those who wish us live
Our life and love—our children.

Please

Please listen when I say my dear

My love for you is quite sincere.

No other girl could ever do

For there is no one else like you.

Your pleasant charms fill my every minute,

And my heart holds your laughter within it.

Your lovely smile completes my day,

Night brings dreams of your tender ways.

Your warm, sweet kiss strengthens my life,

Which I give to you if you'll be my wife

Sing

Sing a song of love to her,
Sweet melodies to charm her heart,
With soft refrains weave magic sounds
To tenderly stir her heart.

Breathe the notes of sweetness, tunes of joy
That await her at your lips;
Then go but now an octave higher,
And sing to her your kiss.

Yet beg her to come near to you,
Pray listen closely dear,
'It's not my heart's slow beat,
But it's my love you hear.'

Yes, listen to my love,
To its dear song pay heed,
'Your heart alone is what I want,
Your love is what I need.'

Yet listen not to my heart's tunes
For tunes are writ by fools;
But listen only to the boy—
    'I love you.'

Night

Night is the sorrow that falls
Like death upon my heart.
No light to see men, but—
Light enough to see myself.
I am a man.
Other men are good.
Other men are happy.
Other men are problem-freed.
But, I do not see other men,
For the dark is all enclosing
In its lonely call.
I call out.
Who answers?
      Despair.
I start.
Who lurks?
      Fear.
What have I to despair, to fear?
Night knows and tells.
It is I.
What am I but a maker of verses?
Poor verses for all the effort.
I mourn my poetic lack.
I fear for my instead life.
In light I am clothed in man's deceits.
At night I am naked.
I bare my soul to my own eyes,
And shudder at its ugliness,
And wait for day to spare me misery,
For a little while longer—
Until night comes again.

Ask Me Why

Ask me why I love you,
I'll not tell you why.
Ask me why I love you,
I may even cry.
Yet, ask me if I love you,
I'll kiss you and reply:
'I love you more than anything,
I know not why.'

Wait and I will try to tell,
Before you turn to go.
Wait and I will try to tell,
Why I love you so.
I.ve searched mu soul for reasons,
And still I do not know
Why you should be the very one
Whom I worship so.

Perhaps your eyes entrance me,
And in their web entwine
With golden streams of sunlight
That tangle mine in thine.
Perhaps your lips allure me
With kisses sweet as red wine,
And in my senseless stupor
Steal this soul of mine.

Or is it your smooth brown tresses
With flowing strands of soft light,
That draw mu soul away6 from me
Like the slowly ebbing tide.
Or is it your tender arms
That drain me of my might,
That leave me tired and restless,
Sleepless for another night.

Ask me why I love you,
I'll tell you not why.
Ask me why I love you, I may even cry.
Yet ask me if I love you,
I'll kiss you and reply:
'I love you more than anything
I know not why.'

Death Comes Early

Death comes early to men like me

On fields of green quite like my home.

Love too comes early to me;

It must or I'll die without.

But even love when it comes,

And it did to me, I know;

Brings a bit of cold to chill

The warmest fire of life.

Love's not always warm and bright.

I shiver, my emotions stiffen.

I turn my collar to the wind,

And walk face to Death's bleak blow.

Yes, I can speak of love and death,

And not be vexed by the unsymmetry;

For, one only focuses the other clearly,

And enhances beauty of love in life.

With death I feel the warmth

Of love forever to be missed—

With love I feel the chill

Of death wished never to come.

Yet I say that death can bear good;

I never wish to lose love again

Now that I've found what I may be

Creator of life through love.

Hear now While I fear chill,

Death, please spare me your storm.

Let me be not cold and unloved,

Only chilled and loved evermore.

What's This?

What's this upon your finger—
Flashing, shining, breathing light,
Living, catches my. I swim,
Then sink, drifting down and down,
Caught in a swirl of color.
Whirling panorama of res, yellows,
Blues, greens—all bright hues—
Sweeps round past my eye; then
Nothing, but white, a light, bright—
So white, I see spots in my
Unaccustomed eyes—dancing spots,
All sizes, all colors, all round.
Again I fall and float and hear
All many sounds sweet to ear.
Oaten flutes treble swift, each reed
Outwhistling the others; fleece-strung lyres
Play harmony, each string singing love.
Now dancing feet of mine touch down—
Grass is good to me. My trip is ended.

   I wake.

Where am I? Have I slept?
No, not quite, I've only dreamed
With eyes awake of you my love.
I've looked into your eyes, then gaze
Upon this ring—the sign I give to you
Of the care and loving thoughts
That always stay with you.
Now let me kiss your soft red lips
To stir my dreams anew.
Then let me rest my love-filled head
Upon your tneder breast.

   I love you.

Had I Life

Had I life, could I die?
I could. Then rise as high
Above me flies a bird winging
To clouds pink. Wink at
The sun and fly do I too,
Above the cloud to find—
      Beauty in many goodly shapes
      Of love. Maidens dance on cloud,
      And beckon me near to hear
      Songs they sing to the birds,
      Now white-fleeced, pure, soft—
      Love, this bird is. I come down
      To touch the bird who flies
      From me to higher, lighter clouds.
      I spring to follow, down I fall
      To earth and—
Birth to man-like life again.
Now there is yet another bird
To see, hear, touch, even grasp
And hold near. I plead
To you pure bird to fly and carry
Me too to your cloud.
      Love me and we'll reach ink clouds,
      And listen to the maidens
      Sing to me of you,
      My Love.
          I love you.

A Leaf—An Ode

A cold wind envigors me,
Sweeps me, swirls upward—leafward.
Blows my mind within and without
The social gathering of other hued leaves,
But never dropping me to earth
Cold, brown, dead like the rest.
Still I float touching close the ground
Then climbing up and above
The gold Autumnal trees of Wisdom.
I've been plucked from the Tree;
Now it's to me and the wind
To keep from falling ignorant, ugly, dead.
Earth affords me rest for sure,
But rest my body only craves.
Mind is alive, mind is free.
I am mind, mind frees me
From the sweet comfort—desire of death.
Earth and sky I behold
With need to touch neither.
See the earth, Its pleasance alluring;
See the sky, its beauty eluding.
I was safe in the tree;
Now I am loose, unsteady.
I do nothing but drift forever,
And my being never succumbs
To the seemed good of earth—it fools.
I am nurtured too well
By Mother, the Wisdom Tree,
To let cold winds blow me down
To earth where I need not be buried.
I need nothing but sweet Aeolus
Play my tuned strings of mind
And create a music of sweetest thought.

Shared by Two

Arms are tender when shared by two,
My embrace to be shared with you.

Nights are warmer when shared by two,
Kisses warmer when shared with you.

Troubles are fewer when shared by two,
Burdens lighter when shard with you.

Life is sweeter when shared by two,
Love is sweeter when shared with you.

Dreams are made to be shared by two,
I dream that I'll share all with you.

Saying Nothing and Everything

January 23, 1969
(You don't need to know how to write to write what you feel; you must only know what you feel. The writing comes from the feeling.)

What good to a man though he toil till dusk
Are the several coins he holds in his hand.
Has he sweated and groaned calloused these
Self same hands that now burn ever so
With flaming pleasure quick to be bought,
And quicker to turn to acrid ash.
What worth is such cyclic nonsense today
To pain one's self with work for nothing
But trifles tossed aside in a day.

Good comes to a man who'd toil till night
To maintain his self and family well
So that he may turn his night thoughts up
To God from whom he came. Came indeed
For labor in fields, to furrow the soil;
To nurture and care for fresh-bloomed buds,
And reap come Harvest the full-filled stocks
Of life's bounteous blessings and God's gifts,
Which last not a day but forever to stay.

Toil's not meant to be bartered for pleasure,
But given in gratis for the strength
God has given—strength to stand and work,
To sweat and to love, to break and exist
In a world made for us. This alone should
Suffice as payment for our labors.
What need of silver meaning little to God.
Words speak to God, it is our way to say
'We labor for love, we ask you no pay.'

I Am From

I am from Good Samaritan Hospital,
Cincinnati's valley awash in Ivory Soap's acerbic smell,
Hoosier born parents, Ohio transplants,
Youngest of four children, only boy

Irish Grandpa Billie of thirteen born back of Shamrock Inn, by tracks,
German Grandma Mayme born hilltop high above town,
German Grandpa Herman farmer rocky terrain Manchester Township
German Grandma Mayme caregiver, farmer Brookville

Mom only child of Sheriff and County Recorder,
Dad oldest son of foundry coreman and homemaker,
Me, three older sisters, two to be nuns, one a free spirit,
Each jealous of me, no hand-me-downs

Old Catholic Church, mission style, white stucco,
Bell tower sitting over oak front door,
Mom and girls walk to early service, home to prepare Sunday meal,
Dad and I ride '47 Merc sedan, noon Mass, aisles standing room only,
Anchored at dining room's old upright piano,
Dad tickles ivories 'Jelly Roll Blues'

I am from Goodman School kindergarten, first grade,
Step dutifully through declared Boys(or Girls) entrance,
Bow obediently to black-wimpled nuns of St. Margaret Mary,
Pray fervently Sister Jean Therese pleased with my work.

Second grade books stashed in metal sliding-door cabinet,

I love books, leaning deep inside,
Little Bobby slams sliding doors, smashes my head,
Good nun introduced me, Dr. Kraus, stitches.

Thirst for printed page slaked in third grade
Happy Birthday 'Fighting Father Duffy' and 'Life of Thomas Aquinas'
Subscription to Young Christian Book of Month Club
Fourth grade Miss Pancera marches class to library,
New world, born 'Adventures of Homer Price'
Oh, for that donut machine again.

Monthly Dayton excursions visit siblings, nuns-to-be,
Two-hours backroads to Salem Heights
Comic books feed boredom, Mom knew all tricks,
Liebrich's Pharmacy stocked 10 cent comics
'Sad Sack', 'Dick Tracy' , 'Fearless Fosdick'

I am from coal truck dumping load in side yard,
Shoveled into coal cellar, hands scrubbed with Fels Naptha
Mom rings clothes from wash machine to utility sink,
Sheets snap in wind on line in backyard.

Snoopy, black and white part collie, part whatever,
Running up down backyard chasing neighbor boys,
Baby alligator sent from Florida Aunt Betty,
Living in basement until it bit Mom

Two-story, square wood-shingled house,
Three second floor windows breathed
 Breeze of huge front yard maple shade tree,
Wood planter under windows, bedroom splashed in spring scents,

Dad after work every other year
Climb, scrape, paint, repeat.

Basement fruit cellar a 60's bomb shelter,
White brick fireplace ceramic gas logs warm mornings,
Nineteen narrow steps up to two big bedrooms,
Three heads in big bed with sisters early,
Dad partitioned one bedroom to two when I turned ten.

I am from dirt paths between houses worn bare kids playing,
Street Wiffle ball—telephone pole foul line, maple tree home run,
Basketball court Smith's driveway, evenings December through March
Transistor radio blared Bearcat Basketball most nights,
WSAI top forty solid sounds serenaded players other nights.

Wagners Furniture red-bricked, huge Savannah-facing show windows,
Color TV eyes pressed against glass, glued to Bonanza Saturday night,
Radels Grocery 2-story brick, apartment over store opposite corner,
Emporium to everything painted, thick-cardboard, real-life portraits
Addictive 1953 Topps baseball cards, pink gum.

Further south down same avenue rests Savannah Café,
Watering hole for thirsty fans of street ballgames
Lugging glass jugs, two fingers snug in loop at the mouth,
No drops spilled, no thirsts unquenched

I am from Christmas Eve rides through holiday-lighted neighborhood,
Ending at Stable in Mt. Healthy, a carrot for donkey,
Miraculous how presents appear under tree upon return,
Stockings hung fill noses scents of nuts, anise, peppermint, citrus

Mothers, Fathers Days, Grandmas Birthday, marked family calendar,

Everyone a dish, Mom's a green depression glass bowl of Potato Salad,
Hands washed, enlisted to help, my jobs, crack eggs, wash potatoes, Critical job, taster, does it need more pickle juice?
Yellowed faded recipe card fails to list most important ingredient...Love.

Were it to be written, Mom's Cook Book
Features list of dishes ladled from Great Depression—
Spam scored, rubbed with brown sugar, peppered with cloves, baked.
Tomato-sauced spaghetti garnished with hot dog slices,
Navy beans, chicken stock, carrots, onions, and ham bone, a soup
Cornmeal, boiling water, salt, chill, slice, fry mush, add maple syrup.

I am from men who smoked, loved beer, worked hard, bowed heads,
Women hand-washed clothes, dishes, cooked, laughed, prayed, walked .
Grandma Fahey never put ear to phone,
Grandpa Fahey pushed off the foundry floor at 72.

Mom walked, balanced checkbook, cooked, never raised her voice ,
I never gave her reason to
Dad worked as Purchasing Agent, lived as a woodworker and Clockmaker,
taught by quiet example

Couple never borrowed a dime they couldn't repay,
Prayed for others.
I am from all of this.

No Elizabeth Barrett and Robert Browning are my wife and I; but there are some yellowed, dog-eared testaments to the elegiac emotions of each being both inspiration and inspired. The next few pages offer proof that the bard's muse tickled Kay's imagination as well as well as mine. Enjoy the work of the trained dietician of the couple, proving that love knows no bounds to the writing of a good verse.

Let Me Wonder

Let me wonder,
Let me love,
Let me wish,
Let me watch—above.

Let me hope,
Let me live,
Let me care,
Let me be—aware.

Let me try,
Let me succeed,
Let me always
Thy graces—heed.

For with thy help
We will win
We will last
We will be—free.

There Once Was

There once was a boy named Fahey

Who never had much to say;

But to me he has spoken

And our love's a firm token,

That'll leave him a preacher to pay.

There once was a handsome young boy

Whose love was perpetually 'coy'

Because of his talent,

She made him be gallant

And found him a <u>tree</u>—mendous joy.

Know I
December 30, 1964

Know I a boy with hair so blond,
Who seems to wave a magic Wand?
Indeed I do, who makes things we do,
Memories to b pondered through and through.

Know I a boy, who seems at first shy,
But underneath vast depths do lie?
Indeed I do, who thinks as I hope
And passes cures to use when I mope.

Know I a boy who is a steadying influence,
When my topsy-turvy world is worth two cents?
Indeed I do, without him my trouble is great,
But with him, I cannot hate but only contemplate.

Know I a boy with a future so bright,
That I fear I'll block its precious light?
Indeed I do, but let me be the girl behind him
To make that light grow brighter and never dim.

Distant
January 23, 1965

Perhaps, from you I seem to roam,

But oddly enough my heart has found its home.

I wonder, seeking to know for myself,

Acting for others was a impish little self.

Each time I return I ponder over life,

Filled with all its selfish daily strife.

Will we last, are you the one for me?

Only time and the hour will let me see.

The fond hopes I hold are distant,

Who knows, maybe we'll always be consistent.

www.ingramcontent.com/pod-product-compliance
Lightning Source LLC
Chambersburg PA
CBHW061335040426
42444CB00011B/2936